IN
EVERYTHING
GIVE
THANKS

And, I mean in
Everything!

For this is
The will of God in Christ Jesus
Concerning you.   I Thessalonians 5:18

KATHIE ANN ENGLISH

A Dedication

To Those I Love
Peter, Becky,
Mark, Mary, & Paul

Thank You for Encouraging Me
to Finish This Book

But You, O Lord,
shall endure forever,
And the remembrance of
Your name to all generations.
Psalm 102:12

Contents

But those who wait on the Lord
Shall renew their strength;
They shall mount up with wings
like eagles,
They shall run and not be weary,

They shall walk and not faint.

Isaiah 40:31

From a Friend

*In everything give thanks, for this is the will of God in Christ
Jesus concerning you. 1 Thessalonians 5:18*

A simple Scripture that many know by heart. But few take it seriously. Few are willing to engage in what is implied "in everything." In this book, *In Everything Give Thanks*, Kathie English brings us to the depths of her experience with God. Journey with her as she encounters life-wrenching realities scarred by physical, emotional, and spiritual afflictions. Afflictions that express the utter anguish and torment emerging from experiences sculptured and shaped by a living and loving God.

See how this life-long divine work created a deep understanding in Kathie's heart of what it truly means to *give thanks for everything*. Discover how God, in love, brought Kathie to a truth to be a model for the rest of us—*in everything give thanks*, no matter how hard, difficult, and seemingly impossible life can be—the good, the bad, and the ugly. This book is worth your time to read and may even change your life.

Kathie and her husband, Peter (now deceased), are special friends with many enjoyable years of shared experiences. My wife, Bev, had a special relationship with Kathie, discipling her into a closer walk with Jesus.

~Don Zoller, 2024

This I recall to my mind,
Therefore I have hope.
Through the Lord's mercies
we are not consumed,
Because His compassions fail not.
They are new every morning;
Great is Your faithfulness.
"The Lord is my portion," says my soul,
"Therefore I hope in Him!"
Lamentations 3:21–24

Forward

My reason for writing this book is to share with others that when God makes a command in His Word, He makes it for our blessing, not our aggravation or frustration. God has promised an abundant life if we adhere to His principles and follow His commands.

When we thank God for all things, we allow Him to work in us. We let Him bless us with His peace because we have obeyed His will. When we give Him thanks in a difficult situation, we give Him room to change us and bring glory to His name. *In everything give thanks, for this is the will of God in Christ Jesus concerning you (I Thessalonians 5:18).*

We do this for no other reason than because God commands us to do so. And I have discovered in giving thanks in obedience, there is joy, which is the fruit of the Holy Spirit.

I will praise the Lord

according to His righteousness,

And will sing praise

to the name of the Lord Most High.

Psalm 7:17

Introduction

I n everything give thanks? Why should I? This is the age of the new morality! I'm supposed to do what pleases me! I deserve a break today! I'm worth it! I owe it to myself. I only live once. I want to enjoy my life; I deserve it! Besides, I've been given a bad deal all my life, why should I give thanks? Everything is always going wrong; nothing ever goes right for me. Anytime I can satisfy me, I'm going to do it! These are the words heard daily. I hear them in commercials, on the street, at the store when I go shopping, and even from those I go to Church with.

But God's Word says, *"In everything give thanks, for this is the will of God in Christ Jesus concerning you." I Thessalonians 5:18*

This isn't a suggestion; this is a command! Not just for the pastor, the deacons, the elders, or the Sunday School teachers, but all Christians everywhere. Our homes, families, friends, country—accidents, bad deals, friendships lost, house robbed, death of those we love, daily hurts, irritations, spills on the white carpet—*give thanks!*

God doesn't ask us to be thankful because of how we feel or based on our emotions, which change from moment to moment. But to give thanks is an act of the *will*, which is part of being willing to be made willing. We begin a healing process of the situation that hurts and pains us so much by giving thanks.

Ever since I wanted to write this book, God has been teaching me that I had to prove what I was writing about. Whenever I give thanks in a difficult situation, the situation constantly changes because attitude is everything! Praise affects our lives when we do it and even when we think it can't make a difference.

This is what this book is all about—giving thanks in any and every situation puts the events into God's hands—the good, the bad, and the ugly! Then, He begins to work that situation out for our good and His glory.

In the following few pages, I would like to share with you some events from my life and the lives of others when, by giving thanks, I placed the responsibility in God's hands. He was able to heal my life and the lives of others and bless us in ways He would never have been able to do if we had not followed His command, *In everything, give thanks.*

Chapter 1

Many Years of Faithfulness

A s I look back over my life, I can see God's faithfulness. I can see His hand upon me even before I was born. God chose to put me into a family that lived by many Biblical principles even though they were not Christians. My parents were high school sweethearts from the time they were sixteen. When Mom graduated from high school, Dad wanted to get married immediately. But Mom said she wanted to get "some kind of education" if she ever needed to go to work. So, she went to business school and worked for the Tacoma News Tribune. Eventually, they married when they were both twenty, two years later.

Dad was Catholic, and Mom was Protestant. My parents were married on June 6, 1942. It was wartime. I am not sure how long it was after they were married that Dad joined the Navy. When he left for the South Pacific, Mom was pregnant with me. While Dad was gone, Mom and I lived with my grandmother, grandfather, and great-grandmother. Boy, was I spoiled!

During this time, sometime between the ages of two and three, my great-grandmother took me to a Nazarene Church about a block from our house. There, I heard the Gospel for the very first time. I only remember attending this church once, but when I heard about God, I knew I wanted to know Him.

I remember a short time after going to the Nazarene Church, Jehovah's Witnesses came to the door. They talked to my grandmother about God. And they left a purple book. After they left, I kept looking at this book to learn about God because they had mentioned His name. But of course, at three I couldn't read.

Dad came home from the war on leave when I was about three. During that time, we moved to our own little house. It was the proverbial little white house with a white picket fence, plus Mommy, Daddy, and baby make three.

Mom said that each Sunday morning early, I would pound on Dad's head, trying to wake him up, saying, "Take me to Sunday School." Mom said that Dad would wake up every Sunday morning with a headache, but she never told him why.

Mom was pregnant again when Dad went back to war in Korea. My brother Steve was born while Dad was gone. I was old enough to be Mom's little helper. We did everything together. We ironed together. I even had my own ironing board and my own little electric iron.

Finally, in grade school, a next-door neighbor invited me to her Methodist Church. I was so excited, and she took me every week. Sometimes even Mom went, too.

When I finished the third grade, we moved to another home in University Place, a suburb of Tacoma. There was another neighborhood church, and Mom took us. We walked. By this time there were four children: me and three younger brothers. I got to sing in the children's choir in this church. When I was in the fifth grade, I asked Mom if I could visit a Catholic church with the next-door neighbors to see what it was like, because Dad was Catholic. She said, "Just this once, but don't ask to go again." Of all the choices I might make, Catholic was not to be one of them when I chose for myself. I never asked to go again. I didn't sense the presence of God I was looking for there.

Another neighbor took my brother Steve and me to vacation Bible school. I went forward when they gave the altar call. Mom was so angry. She said I embarrassed her so much for doing that.

The summer before the sixth grade, we moved to Olympia. That October, Dad took us to Lacey to the nearest church, which happened to be a Bible-believing "preaching-the-Gospel" kind of church. It also had a Sunday School bus ministry. My brothers and I went to Sunday School every week after that. They picked us up and brought us home. The people there reached out to us. I knew that what they had was what I wanted. I began to be convicted about my sinful and rebellious nature.

By human standards, I hadn't done anything too terrible, but by God's standards, I was a sinner in need of a Savior. I began to realize that if I were going to become a Christian, I would have to make some sacrifices. I also realized there would be some persecution, and it was going to start at home, where I was cared for and loved very much.

I began to realize that even though my parents gave me the choice of what kind of religion I wanted, being totally sold out to Jesus Christ was not what they had in mind. They didn't want me living a life that would convict them of their sin while I followed my convictions.

At the age of twelve, I knew that all I had heard about Jesus was what I wanted, but there was one more obstacle in my way. I loved to dance! For some people dancing is probably okay, but dancing was a *god* in my life at that time. I lived to dance! Every opportunity to dance again was all I thought about. Dancing was also very important to my parents as well. They had won dance contests when they were younger. Mom was into ballet and tap dance and they wanted me to do the same.

In the eighth grade there was to be a *Tolo Dance* where the girl invited the boy. On the day of the dance, the boy I had invited came down with chicken pox. My friends convinced me that I should go to the dance anyway. While I was at the dance, the Holy Spirit kept speaking to me all evening about choosing whom I should serve on this day. Who did I want to be my god, Jesus or dancing? And there, on the dance floor on April 18, 1958, I surrendered my life to the Lord Jesus Christ.

My life changed dramatically at this point, just like I knew it would. I joined a teenage Bible club that year. They had a Bible memorization contest. The first prize was to go to Black Lake Bible Camp for a week. We had to memorize fifty verses. I came in second place and my friend got first place. She couldn't go to camp, so we traded prizes. She got the Bible, and I got to go to camp. It was the best thing that could have happened to me as a new believer of only four months. Because I was from a non-Christian home, I thought I had arrived in heaven when I got there. It didn't matter that I knew no one in my cabin. I knew the Lord and spent the week going to every prayer meeting and Bible study the camp offered.

It was there at Black Lake Bible Camp at the campfire I dedicated my life to the Lord on August 24, 1958. At this time, I took Isaiah 40:31 as my life verse.

But they that wait upon the Lord shall renew their strength; they shall mount up with wings as eagles, they shall run and not be weary, they shall walk and not faint.

And this verse has proved over and over to me to be a source of my physical, spiritual, and emotional strength.

When I returned home, Mom mentioned how much I had changed in one week. When I tried to share the Lord with her, she became angry. "What do you think I am anyway, a heathen?" When I didn't answer right away, she became angrier. From that point on she tried to put every barrier she could in my way to keep me from the Bible or church. But God was on my side. Every time I prayed, He provided a way. If I were found reading my Bible, Mom would find something *better* for me to do.

I began having my quiet times with the Lord in the bathtub behind locked doors. Being the only girl among three brothers I was allowed this privacy. Before I was a believer, I was always encouraged to go to church. Now I was told I didn't need to go. It wasn't necessary. Someday I would forget this foolishness. But I continued to hunger and thirst for righteousness even more.

In high school, I grew in the Lord and looked forward to every opportunity to hear His Word or be with others who knew God. I would attend the Wednesday night prayer meetings.

Sometimes, I would be the only one under forty, but I didn't care about age. I just had this longing to get to know God better. I read every book the pastor had in his library except for his concordances and study books.

In April 1962, my senior year of high school, I talked with Dad about his need for a Savior. Yes, Dad was Catholic, but to my knowledge I had only seen him go to church a few times during my lifetime. He said he respected what I believed but that he would never change. Two weeks later, at the age of forty, Dad died.

For a short time, I was angry at God for taking Dad. He was the one that I was the closest to, and he was the one who allowed me the freedom to go to church. Why didn't God take Mom? But as I look back now, I can see that Mom had the tender heart toward spiritual things. She was under great conviction. She wasn't saved. Yet, finally, after almost forty years, she admitted that Jesus was the One she needed.

When Dad died, Mom became an alcoholic overnight. She told me that my brothers and I no longer mattered to her. She began staying out all night and coming home at 6:00 am in time to get ready to go to work. (Mom had gone to work when I was fourteen). My grandmother lived two houses away from us and tried to help in any way she could. She tried to talk some sense into Mom's new lifestyle, but Mom told her she didn't have to answer to anyone.

During this time, I was deciding what college to go to. I wanted to attend Seattle Pacific College, a Christian liberal arts university. I had visited there for a high school preview weekend the previous February. As a result of Dad's death, there were funds available for me to go to college, but Mom said I couldn't go to a Christian College, so I ended up going to Western Washington State College in Bellingham. She said I would receive no money for school if I chose anything else.

I really didn't want to go away from home after Dad had died. I was grieving for Dad, but no one in the family seemed to care. They just seemed to want me out of the way at college. It wasn't until the end of October, my freshman year of college, that I finally cried over Dad's death. I cried for a week, non-stop. At the time of his death, I was making funeral arrangements and caring for three younger brothers, ages fourteen, ten, and eight, because Mom had forgotten she was a mom.

I had been a good student in high school, but I barely passed my classes in my first year of college. My grade point average dropped from 3.5 to 1.2. Many people from my home church prayed for me and wrote me encouraging letters. I received about ten letters a day. Gradually, Mom began to change back to the one I had known as a child, but she never quit drinking. This was probably the most challenging year of my Christian life.

I lived in a dorm where I knew no Christians. I was able to get to church once a week. A bus came from The Firs Church. I joined Inter-Varsity Christian Fellowship, a Bible study for college students. I thoroughly examined my walk with God that year. It seemed all uphill. It would have been so easy to become like the crowd I lived with, but I could not. My roommate tried everything she could to discredit my testimony. She told me later that she did it because she was under such great conviction. She became a Christian shortly after school was out that year.

In my second year of college, I lived at home. I went to Centralia College. My grades went back up again. This year, my grandfather died, and I was very close to him. He lived only two doors away. My uncle, who lived next door, died of cancer practically overnight. All the people I dearly loved were dying. This year was even harder. But the Lord was there through it all causing me to cling to Him more tightly.

In March 1964, overwhelmed by the loss of those I loved, the domestic issues at home, and *spring fever*, I was tired of school. At the end of the quarter, I quit. I went to work for a wealthy family, cleaning their house and taking care of their two boys, ages four & five. But what I really wanted was my own house and my own children. However, God had not yet provided that for me.

On May 9, 1964, while working for this wealthy family, my brother came and brought me a truck to get home later. He brought a friend with him that he wanted me to meet. My brother was almost four years younger than me. I was twenty, so I was assuming his friend was about sixteen. His friend was not sixteen. His friend was twenty. My brother had been trying to cross my path with this "friend" for almost two years without any success. So, finally, very frustrated, he just brought him to me. That friend was Peter, my husband-to-be. The next day,

Sunday, was my day off. He came over that afternoon to borrow my brother's tools to fix his car.

Peter liked to fish, or so he said. We lived on a lake. My brother again *made arrangements* with me to row while Peter fished. So I did because I liked to row, and my brother knew this. After five or six weeks of rowing almost every evening and on Saturdays and Sundays, Peter asked if he could take me out because of all the rowing I had done. I said, "No, I row because I like to row." He said, "Let me start over. Will you go out with me just because I want to take you out?" I said, "Yes."

During our dating, Peter attended church with me every Sunday. I asked him if he was a Christian. He said "Yes," so I thought I could date him without any problem. I was still a new believer and from a non-Christian home. No one questioned my dating him. He was kind and considerate, good to his family and mine. And I was falling in love with him. Family was important to him, and he loved children. But the question I never asked him was, do you love Jesus? Since Peter was from Germany, one is either Catholic or Lutheran. He wasn't Catholic, so therefore, in his mind, he was a Christian.

Throughout our dating months, his and my brothers were always with us. What I didn't know was that during all these weeks Peter was paying my brother for any information that he could get from me about how I felt about him. I also didn't know Mom, grandmother, and my three brothers wanted me to marry Peter. But no one said anything about it. Finally, Peter told Steve he would propose on Christmas 1964. But Peter couldn't wait.

On the Fourth of July 1964, he proposed while we were on one of our "boat trips. He said, "If I asked you to marry me, what would you say?" I said, "Yes. What did you think I would say?" He was so sure I would say, "No," that he was silent for half an hour. My brother was furious that night when he came to pump me for information like he usually did so he could relay it to Peter. But the deal was over. No more money! My brother got his first car out of the deal—this information service.

On July 28, I got my engagement ring. We were officially engaged. We went to our pastor and asked if he would marry us. He said, "Yes." We got together for pre-marriage counseling several times. But the interesting thing was he continued to question Peter about his salvation and kept repeating he would never marry a Christian to a non-Christian. It was like the Holy Spirit was telling Peter he was not saved. But because children attend one hour of Bible class every school day in Germany, he knew all the right answers.

I don't think even Peter knew he was unsaved at that point, but I was beginning to suspect it. I would ask Peter to pray with me about our future and wedding. He would always say "You pray first and then he would pray. On December 4, 1964, we were married. About six weeks after we were married Peter asked Jesus into his heart at the evening service the last Sunday of January 1965. He didn't go forward during the service, but I sensed a greater tenderness toward spiritual things afterward. This was another time when God was faithful to me when I was not faithful to Him.

During our first six years of marriage, I had four miscarriages and four live births. All, by the time I was twenty-six. I had four kids under four. I finally had the husband, children, and home I longed for. These were happy years, although they were not always easy years. During this time, Peter was out of work four times, four months each.

We learned to depend on the Lord for everything—every penny. Sometimes we prayed for food, sometimes for shoes, sometimes for pajamas, and God always supplied. I remember one friend always tried to talk me into getting a job. I had worked at a bank the first year we were married, but the thought of leaving my children to someone else's care did not appeal to me. God had given me these lives to shape for eternity. I could not leave that to someone else. I told my friend that when I needed something, I would just talk to my Heavenly Father and He would send it in a paper sack. He did this over and over during those first six years. *In everything give thanks.*

In 1973, we had a lot of sickness in our house. From March to August, it seemed we had every disease known to man. We started with croup, then mumps, measles, chicken pox, and finally meningitis.

Paul came down with meningitis. We didn't know that's what he had. On Friday, we went in for a throat culture, but it would take a week to come back. I couldn't get him to take any liquids. So, I thought popsicles would work. Even that didn't appeal to this two-year-old. So, after he had taken a few licks, his sister decided she would eat it for him, which meant she was exposed to whatever he had.

On Sunday night he went to sleep. But on Monday morning he did not wake up. I kept trying. Then he would cry out sounding like a wild bobcat, which is one of the symptoms of meningitis—high fever, wild cries, and refusal to take water.

On Tuesday, I called the doctor. He had me bring him in right away. He did a spinal tap, and I could hear his cries echoing all over Memorial Clinic. I didn't want to be in the room when they did this. The doctor came out and said he had meningitis and a 50/50 chance of living. I remember the tears jumping out of my eyes forward onto the floor rather than sliding down my face.

Paul was immediately taken over to St. Peters Hospital. He was in the hospital about three or four days when the nurse said we've done all we can do. He's going to die. At this time, our church had been praying around the clock for us. I could feel it. I then called our pastor and told him what the nurse had said.

I went out to the car to take a break. I usually came to the hospital at 9:00 am every morning when Paul woke up and stayed until 9:30 pm each evening or until he went to sleep. Walking to the car, I told the Lord, "If you want him, you can take him. He's yours. You know what is best for our family. As I opened the car door, Paul's Sunday School paper fell out on the ground. His verse for the week was I Peter 5:7, *Cast all your cares upon Him, for He cares for you.* I really needed to hear that. I went back to the hospital an hour later.

When I returned to the hospital, the nurse came up to me and said, "I'm not sure exactly what happened, but while you were gone, Paul took a turn for the better. He's going to live! God had only wanted my surrender, not my child. God is always faithful in doing what is best for us.

During this time, Mark and Mary, our other two children, came down with chicken pox while Paul was in the hospital. Mae and Duane Summers took them to their home and cared for them. Becky, the one who ate Paul's infected popsicle, also came down with a mild case of meningitis, but she didn't have to go to the hospital.

God, in His faithfulness, provided people and their prayers to help in every way possible. After Paul came home from the hospital, God provided Linda Sommers to help me each day. Paul had to learn to walk and talk all over again. He was two and a half years old, but now only the size of an eight-month-old baby. But within a month, he was walking, talking, and gaining the weight he needed. God had given us back our son. *In everything give thanks.*

During the next ten years of marriage, we were busy with the normal activities of family life. We were involved in many church activities: teaching Sunday School, Wednesday night "Jet Cadets," choir, showers, church socials, and entertaining visiting missionaries in our home.

The annual missions conference always fell when we had the least money and food. It seemed like we always had to squeeze the chickens for eggs and pray for every meal on the table while the missionaries stayed those four days with us. We started supporting missionaries early in our marriage. Being involved in missions was one of our greatest joys.

We were also involved in 4-H with our kids for many years. Peter and I were both 4-H leaders. During this busy time, God stopped me in my tracks with pneumonia. It was February. While I was in bed, I had time to read. Anne Ortlund's book *Disciplines of the Beautiful Woman* was one of the books I read. One of the questions asked in the book was, "Are you so busy for God that you don't have enough time with God?" God now stopped me spiritually—right in my tracks.

Shortly after this time, a woman came into my life to disciple me. She met with me four hours once a week for two and a half years. I began the slow-down process of understanding what following Jesus truly means. I would like to quote from Anne Ortlund's book,

Unless we are rich in God and His Word, our spiritual lives will be thin, and we will have nothing of eternal significance to contribute to our fellow Christians. Our giving or serving will be like pouring out of an empty pitcher.

Another quote from her book,

If all of our life is visible to others, from the time we get up in the morning until we fall into bed at night, then we'll be an unsteady as a ship without a keel. Indeed, the more of us that is invisible, hidden from the world in quiet, in study, in planning, and in prayer, the more effective our visible life will be.

In 1983, we began attending Westwood Baptist Church. I was still recovering from a three-and-a-half-month bout with food poisoning. This was another time when God stopped me in my tracks and said, "Slow down." *Be still and know that I am God (Psalm 46:10)*. I came very close to dying, but God in His grace had another plan.

The first year we were at Westwood, I didn't take on any responsibilities. Since I like to do anything and everything, this was very difficult for me. But I felt God wanted me just to watch and pray. That was my ministry for that year. I took the church directory and prayed through it once every other week. As I got to know people and their needs, I would make a note of that. I tried to get to know two new people each week and remember their names. Throughout this year, I was learning to be still and wait on God, which is difficult for a *Martha* personality who likes to be "busy with many things."

During this time, I attended Bible Study Fellowship taught by Jan Lapp. She talked about how she would spend a whole day or even an entire weekend with God once a month. At the time, I thought, "What would I do with a whole day with God?" Now, years later, I think it would be a wonderful thing to do. I have tried it, and it is great.

Throughout the next ten years, I got involved in discipling one-on-one ministry and teaching Pioneer Girls. I then took training to teach Precept Bible Studies. I went with two other ladies to Seattle for the three-day training in the spring of that year. I was to teach in the fall. On September 12, I taught the introduction class. I was really excited about teaching the class. But again, God had another plan.

On September 16, 1989, a Saturday night, our son Paul was in an accident. It was serious. A train collided with the car that he and three other students were riding in. The driver of the car tried to beat the train at a crossing. The pavement was wet. The car ended up on the tracks in front of the train. Two students were injured, and one was killed. The driver wasn't hurt. He jumped out before the train hit the car. . .

The story doesn't end here. I invite the reader to read Chapter 2 to see how God, in His faithfulness, handles tragedy.

Ten years later, on August 5, 1999, another event occurred involving my daughter, Becky. Yes. It was another accident. This time it was a head-on collision. Like Paul's accident, it was severe. Once again, God's faithfulness was revealed. Read Chapter 3 to see how.

Throughout the many years of God's faithfulness, through times of turmoil, trials, and tragedies, I learned what it meant to give thanks *in everything.*

Creator of our days,
You know the path ahead,
Trials, troubles abound,
Yet, perfectly arranged
For our blessing and your glory.
One thing is assured,
"I will never leave you nor forsake you.
My love for you can do no other,
I am forever, yes, forever faithful.
I am your God."
Ref: Deuteronomy 7:9

~ Anonymous

Chapter 2

The Train Accident

It was Sunday morning. Peter and I were just about to go out the door to church. It was 9:00 am, and for a change, we were on time! Then the phone rang. No one calls us on Sunday morning. Who could that be?

The person on the phone said, "This is Dr. Pugach in Canada at the Langley Hospital. We'd like permission to operate on your son Mark, I mean Paul."

"Which is it, Mark or Paul? I have sons by both names." I asked. The doctor said, "I don't know why I said Mark, but Paul needs the surgery." "What's wrong with him?" I began to think the worst.

He said, "Didn't the State Patrol call you last night?"

"No, they didn't," I replied.

"Well, this is Dr. Pugach, and I am a plastic surgeon. Your son was in an accident last night—a car collision with a train on the way back to his dorm. A group of college kids went to the Dairy Queen, and it happened on the way back. May I operate? We'd like to begin to operate right away."

"Yes," I said.

He did not tell us the extent of Paul's injuries, so we didn't know exactly what happened until we got to Canada.

After hanging up the phone and explaining to Peter what had happened, we made a few phone calls, asking people to pray. We left immediately for Canada. It was a *very* long three-hour and fifteen-minute drive. We still didn't have any of the details of the accident. We didn't know how badly Paul was hurt or if anyone else was hurt.

We arrived at Trinity Western College, where Paul attended school about 12:30 pm. Mark's former roommate saw us come into the building and came to talk to us. He told us as much as he knew about the accident and that one of the girls riding in the car, Tammy Heide, was dead. She had been run over by the train because she got out on the wrong side of the car. This came as a real shock. I turned white and almost passed out. Then, one of the students took us to the hospital in the next city, about forty-five minutes away. We were told the rest of the story when we arrived at the hospital.

The train had hit the back of the car. Paul had been catapulted from the car's passenger side through the driver's side and across a field two hundred yards. His body was near a river when they found him. His teeth had been knocked out—eight bottom teeth missing, which were lying on his tongue with a smashed jaw. There was a large cut from one side of his face to the other and a six-inch slit across the chin area. A piece of skin ripped off his back the size of a basketball. Both legs and his knees were damaged. With a dislocated shoulder, his left arm hung at his side. The doctor also said that Paul had brain damage and would, in time, need corrective brain surgery. He noted that Paul looked like a badly wounded warrior—like an old man in an eighteen-year-old body.

It took us a while to find Paul. After almost an hour of searching, we found him. It was so good to see that he was alive even though he had been hurt very badly. He was still talking and even smiling. They had a bandage wrapped around his head under his chin like they used to do with cases of mumps. It looked like it was holding his head together. Paul was in good spirits, and we could talk with him and learn firsthand what happened.

Surgery was scheduled for 9:30 am on Sunday. However, other emergencies were worse than Paul's, so his surgery was not until 7:00 pm that night. We spoke with the plastic surgeon before he went into surgery. He was the one we talked to on the phone that morning.

Paul went into surgery. We spent the next four hours waiting and praying. We were so glad that he was still alive. At 11:30 pm, the doctor came out of the operating room and said the surgery had been a success. We were so thankful to the Lord.

We went to the ABC Motel and were grateful for a good night's sleep. Peter would be returning to Olympia the next day. I stayed in Canada with Paul until he was ready to travel back to Olympia.

On Monday, Peter joined me, and we returned to the hospital to visit Paul. A friend of ours, Bob Drohman, came to visit Paul and took Peter back to Olympia. I stayed at the hospital until 9:00 pm and returned to Dr. and Mrs. Snyder's each night. Mrs. Snyder waited for me each night with tea, cookies, and fruit. Because Paul's hospital was in the next city, almost one hour away, I usually got to their home between 10:00–11:00 pm.

Most nights, I had no dinner because Paul got nervous whenever I left the room for anything. He was in constant pain in a strange hospital, in a strange city, with unfamiliar doctors, in a foreign country, and with English accents. This only added to his anxiety. So, returning to the Snyder's, tea and treats were most welcomed.

Once again, the God of all peace was ever present with us during that time. We could feel the prayers of family and friends and the peace that passes all understanding. Everyone from the college was very supportive during this time and encouraged us in many ways. The college president offered their home for me to stay in while I remained in Canada until Paul was released from the hospital in Vancouver.

Paul was released from the hospital on Thursday morning and went home to Olympia. Eventually, we returned to the college in Canada to get his things, which took a little while. Paul wanted to go to the 11:00 am chapel service before going home. As we walked through the door, 1200 students were singing, "*Amazing Grace, how sweet the sound that saved a wretch like me.*" At the sound of those words, Paul and I both burst into tears. I ran back to the car sobbing, realizing just how true those words were in Paul's case. He could have been dead like Tammy. But he was still alive because God had a plan for Paul's life—a life still ahead of him. At that moment, I was very thankful to God for sparing his life again! Many years have passed since then, but I still get tears whenever I hear the song *Amazing Grace.*

The following eight or nine months were filled with daily doctor appointments, surgeries, and therapy treatments. My days were filled with caring for him, which I was only too glad to do. When his jaw was crushed, it damaged most of the nerves in his face, which turned out to be a blessing because he didn't have to take a lot of painkillers. Paul is still healing both inside and out. Because of the accident and the girl who was killed, he had many court hearings during this time. This was a very traumatic time as he rehearsed the same path of the accident each time he met with the lawyer.

Many adjustments were needed to *our* new life—mine and Paul's. Paul needed much care. I first canceled almost all my ministry activities for the next four months. I didn't have time for them. My days were filled with caring for Paul. He needed help with everything: putting on clothes, ice packs on his back, taking the medicines he had to take, and making meals in the blender because his mouth was wired shut. He couldn't use his left arm at all at first. It just hung straight down. Doctor visits for therapy and surgeries, five days a week was our life for months. Paul couldn't drive for many months because of the damage to his knees and arm.

When Paul was able, we began going to the lawyer in Canada. The boy driving the car was suing Paul for damages, saying the accident was Paul's fault. The trips to the lawyer, the doctors, and the psychologist went on for many months. Paul had lots of nightmares during this time. He couldn't sleep till it was almost morning. He also had short-term memory loss for about one year. Paul couldn't remember to take his lunch with him to work and couldn't remember where he was going unless I wrote it down on a sticky note.

In January 1990, Paul returned to Trinity Western College in Canada but had a miserable semester. Because of short-term memory loss, he couldn't concentrate or remember anything he studied. Before the accident, he had a photographic memory. He went from being an 'A' student to a 'D' student. He also had to come home almost every weekend for doctor's appointments. He was lonely and very miserable.

About a year or so after the accident, someone suggested he go to a psychiatrist. I think it was the insurance company. He had to go to one Canadian doctor, and for a second opinion, we took him to a Christian psychologist. He had him write a letter to Tammy, the girl who had died in the accident. He was told to tell her how he felt about the whole deal. Many of the nightmares from the accident stopped after he wrote this letter to her. After 35 years, Paul is still healing, inside and out.

We spent the next three years going to doctors, lawyers, psychologists, psychiatrists, dentists, and surgeries. We spent many hours on the road together. When you spend this much time together, you either hate each other or become very good friends who talk about anything and everything. I think it was during this time Paul and I became good friends.

The passage in the New Testament that talks about our children when they grow up to be our friends came true during this time. I praise God for our friendship. We had a good relationship as parents and child all his growing up years. It was something I really worked at with all my children and has turned out to be a great blessing to my four children to be my best friends. It was worth every minute, every dime, every prayer invested in their lives. *In everything give thanks.*

Yea, though I walk through the valley
of the shadow of death,
I will fear no evil;
For You are with me;
Your rod and Your staff,
they comfort me.
Psalm 23:4

Though the fig tree may not blossom,
Nor fruit be on the vines;
Though the labor of the olive may fail,
And the fields yield no food;
Though the flock may be cut off from the fold,
And there be no herd in the stalls,
Yet I will rejoice in the Lord,
I will joy in the God of my salvation.
Habakkuk 3:17–18

Chapter 3

Becky's Accident

It was a beautiful summer morning, Thursday, August 5, 1999. Becky, my daughter who lived down the road from us, came over with her three children: Kyle, Kelly, and Kayla. We were going to the Thurston County Fair together. We would meet my other daughter, Mary, and her son, Connor, at the fair. Becky would leave her car at my house and ride with me.

We went to the fair and had a wonderful time together. Becky and I won second place in the parent/child "look-alike" contest. It was also Kid's Day at the fair, so the children got in for $1.00. We always enjoyed going to the county fair because we always saw people we hadn't seen for a long time. That day we saw many of our friends—old and new.

At 3:00 pm, Becky had to leave and go to work. She took Kyle and Kayla with her. I told her she could drive to my house, and I would stay at the fair. Peter would come back and meet me there when he got off work. Kelly got to stay with me because it was his turn to spend the night.

As we said our "goodbyes" to Becky, Kyle, and Kayla while they were walking away, Mary said, "Are you going to let Becky drive your new car?" I said, "Why not? She's a good driver." As I said those words, I felt in my heart that something bad was about to happen. Being an optimist by nature, I'm not given to unhealthy fears. But I knew at that moment something was about to happen. For the next two hours, Kelly, Mary, Connor, and I enjoyed the fair.

Mary left the fair at about 5:00 pm. Peter was to meet Kelly and me between 5:00-5:30 pm. Suddenly, the weather changed, and the wind began to blow. Lightning, thunder, and pouring down rain were upon us. Kelly and I stood under a tree to get out of the rain. Then, I heard the public address system calling my name to come to the information booth.

Immediately, I knew Becky and the kids had been in a car accident before I even got the news. I went to the information booth. Paul, our son, was on the phone telling me that a 4x4 truck had gotten into Becky's Lane and hit them head-on! Becky was going downhill, and the truck was coming up the hill very fast. The children got burns from the seatbelt. Other than that, the children were not hurt. Becky was alive because of the airbags and the mighty hand of God.

Becky's feet and legs were caught under the dashboard, and she was hanging out of the car when Peter and Paul arrived before the ambulance. A man came by and asked her who he should call, and she said it was her dad because he was waiting for her to come home. I cried and cried as Paul relayed the message. He said he'd come to the fair and pick us up. The fair traffic and the storm kept him from getting there anytime soon. He was only fifteen minutes away, but it took him one hour to get there.

We went to the hospital. It was not a happy time. Steve, Becky's husband, was angry with me for letting Becky drive our car. He never came out and said it, but his looks toward me were very accusing.

The doctor said she had two broken legs, a left crushed foot, a right broken foot, ankle, and knee—*she would never walk again!* Kyle and Kayla had seatbelt burns, but that was all. They were all still alive. Praise the Lord.

When difficulty strikes, things that are truly important surface: God, people, and relationships are indeed what's important. God, people, and relationships get us through these difficult times. Our relationship with God and our Christian friends helped in so many ways.

Each morning before going to visit Becky at the hospital, about forty people called before 10:00 am. Caring people, praying people, concerned people, and asking what they could do to help. I would jump into the shower each morning crying out to God and praying for strength for the day. Then, I would call Becky, read the Bible to her, and pray with her.

Through all of this, I knew God could be trusted. He is sovereign overall. He never makes mistakes. He uses everything in our lives to draw us closer to Him. He uses circumstances, His Word, and the prayers of family and friends to cause us to realize our need for dependence on Him. Even though I didn't know the outcome, I knew I could give thanks in all things. I had trusted God before, and I knew He could be trusted again. Becky was to go through three more surgeries before the week was over.

First, Becky was at St. Peter's Hospital and then moved to Mother Joseph's, a nursing home facility, and then back to the hospital for more surgery. Finally, she was transferred back to Mother Joseph's, where she stayed for almost a month. On August 26, her wedding anniversary, Becky was still in the nursing home. She and Steve had a candlelight dinner for two in the pavilion at Mother Joseph's. The day before Becky left Mother Joseph's, her sister and friends gave her a surprise thirty-third birthday party in the beautifully landscaped yard. There were fifty people in attendance.

Steve's parents came the day after the accident and took the children to their home in Aberdeen, Washington, for a month. They came with the children once a week to visit Becky. They were a blessing from heaven. With the list of things Becky gave me to do each day, such as taking care of Oma, my mother-in-law, and working for our painting business, I could not have cared for the kids, too. During this time, Steve's parents were such an encouragement to me. When the kids came back, it was time for school to start.

On September 4, 1999, Becky moved into our home to be cared for until she could return home. We had to hire a caregiver because Becky needed someone full-time to take care of her. She couldn't walk and needed to be lifted in and out of bed to use the restroom, shower, and everywhere.

Steve was angry during Becky's recovery. He was angry at God for taking away his wife. He was angry at me for letting her drive my car. He was angry at Peter—I don't know why. He didn't like having to take full responsibility for his family. He liked letting others shoulder the load. But Steve would learn through all this that God was using this for all our good.

Janine Lugenbeel was hired to care for Becky. She and Becky already knew each other. Janine had cared for her brother off and on for many years. He was a quadriplegic. What a blessing Janine was to all of us. We were able to laugh a lot and cry a lot. Her tender care of Becky as she washed Becky's feet daily and cared for the wounds on her legs was a blessing to watch. She was a real encouragement to Becky every day she came to care for her. She went above and beyond the call of duty. It was a real ministry.

The doctor said she would never walk again, but we have an all-powerful God. Nothing is too difficult for Him. He is our *Jehovah–Rapha*, the God who heals, the great physician. We prayed that she would walk by Christmas. On December 23 at our family Christmas Eve, she could walk! Now, twenty-five years later, she walks with only a slight limp.

So many good things came because of the accident. The Bible says,

And we know that God causes all things to work together for good to those who love God, to those who are called according to His purpose. For whom He foreknew, He also predestined to become conformed to His image of His Son that He might be the first born among many brethren. Romans 8:28, 29. (NASB)

For Thou hast tried us, O God; Thou hast refined us as silver is refined. Psalms 66:10 (NASB)

We never know what God will use to refine us as silver. Becky was going through great physical pain. The rest of the family was going through great emotional pain because she was hurting so much.!

We saw how God was caring for our needs. Many people brought meals to our home during Becky's recovery. They did this for several months, serving our family of eight. With each meal, they brought words of encouragement. Even the kids got off the bus in front of our house each afternoon—Kayla came home at noon because she was in kindergarten. Their school, South Bay School, provided what was needed for Becky's children with backpacks filled with school supplies. We saw what seemed to be little conveniences to most as provisions from our mighty God in our time of need.

Becky changed as well through all her trials. She began running to God in a way I'd never seen before. Becky spent hours growing in her walk with God, and it began to show. She needed that spiritual strength to deal with her children and her angry husband each day. I was always amazed as I saw her spend time with each child daily, her love for them, teaching them spiritual truths, disciplining them in love, and praying with them. So much was learned just by watching her. One day, she was complaining about someone with their child. I said, "You used to do that before your accident." She couldn't believe it. God changed her in so many ways.

Because of Steve's anger toward me, I became angry towards him because I had to take care of his responsibilities. He refused to do them. God began to deal with me. I faced the fact that I needed to ask Steve's forgiveness. After I did this, things changed in me. Steve began to change, too. Peter also asked for forgiveness, and Steve told Peter he was sorry.

Steve began to appreciate what Becky really meant to him and how much she did for him. He began to change and do what husbands should do when they love their wives.

We also had a lot of fun days together. Becky and I have always enjoyed our time together. We did a lot of baking together, watched Christmas movies, and made Christmas gifts. Mark flew home from Europe to see his sister. Even at the hospital we enjoyed a time of fellowship with Peter, me, Becky, Mark, Mary, and Paul. Our original family was together again!

Yes, the accident resulted in many good things. It showed us what was really in our hearts, where our faith was, and Who our faith was in. It showed us the motives of our hearts in our relationships with one another.

God, our Great Physician, was again able to display His mighty power by allowing Becky to walk again when the doctor said it wouldn't happen. Even the doctors were amazed and had a meeting to review everything that had happened.

Becky learned to discipline her children in a godly manner and was getting good results as well. Becky and Steve's marriage grew stronger. Becky and Steve were able to move into a bigger house that was adequate for their family and Becky's business.

I grew very close to my grandchildren after having them live with us for almost five months. We discovered how wonderful and giving our friends were as they prayed, gave of their time, brought meals, gifts, flowers, books, cards, calls, visits—anything and everything they could do to make our lives easier.

It is now twenty-five years later, and Becky still walks with a limp occasionally and has had a few more surgeries, but we praise God that she is still physically walking and still walking spiritually with the Lord. *In everything give thanks.*

Those who sow in tears shall reap in joy.
He who continually goes forth weeping,
Bearing seed for sowing,
Shall doubtless come again with rejoicing,
Bringing his sheaves with him.
Psalm 126:5–6

Chapter 4

The Power of Praise

I attended a women's Sunday School class. The teacher, Mrs. Reese, asked the class to share what had been going on in their lives lately. These were praise reports! So, here I am. Struggling to share something. I knew the Lord was teaching me the power of praise the hard way! But I didn't want to share that. This is how learning to praise started.

In 1971, Peter began his own business. I knew when he started his business, he would be working long hours and be gone many hours. I planned activities that would take up the long hours: sewing, writing letters, reading, and taking short trips with the children.

Then, I listened to what the devil had to say about all these hours spent alone. I began to think: Peter doesn't care about us anymore; he doesn't really mind being away from us fourteen hours a day, six days a week; he likes being gone. He wouldn't even miss me if I was gone. I forgot he took time off in May and took us on a nine-day vacation to California, two camping trips, and Sunday picnics when he could have been resting.

All I could do for days was think of everything wrong about him and how unfair it was for me to have total care of the children while he worked. All the time I was doing this, I knew it was wrong, but I continued to wallow in my self-pity. As my friend Barbara said, I was having myself a nice little "pity party." It is a funny thing about self-pity; nobody else seems to really feel sorry for you. They don't need to because I was doing such a good job of it myself. I knew eventually I would have to thank the Lord for the situation, but I just wasn't ready yet.

And so, it was on this Sunday morning, when everyone shared what the Lord had done, I felt miserable. All that next week, each day was worse than the day before. But on Wednesday night, after the prayer meeting, when I came home, I decided to write down everything I had to be thankful for, including my husband, family, and friends. I thanked God for the situation that I was now in because I knew He had something to teach me through it, but I wasn't sure I wanted to learn anything.

I began reading I Corinthians 13:4-7.

Love is very patient and kind, never jealous or envious, never boastful or proud, never haughty or selfish or rude. Love does not demand its own way. It is not irritable or touchy. It does not hold grudges and will hardly even notice when others do it wrong. It is never glad about injustice but rejoices whenever truth wins out. If you love someone you will be loyal to him no matter what the cost. You will always believe in him, always expect the best of him, and always stand your ground in defending him. (TLB)

As I read this, I felt I had lost on all counts. I had really failed as a wife. And yet, I felt like I didn't know where to start. When I returned to class the following week, everyone was praising the Lord again. I felt so far removed from those in this class. I was really in a state of depression.

I read in Colossians 2:6,7:

And now just as you trusted Christ to save you, trust Him too for each day's problems, live in vital union with Him. Let your roots grow down into Him and draw up nourishment from Him. See that you go on growing in the Lord and become strong and vigorous in the truth you were taught. Let you lives overflow with the joy and thanksgiving for all He has done. (TLB)

These verses sounded terrific, but how to attain this sounded impossible. I borrowed Tim La Hay's book, *How to Deal with Depression*, and a book by Francis Gardner Hunter called *Praise the Lord Anyway* and thought maybe these would help. I decided to read a chapter of each of these books after my devotions each morning.

When I looked into the book on depression, I saw in the index there were two chapters on self-pity. I thought this was the book for me. I turned to the chapters on self-pity. First, it said to face self-pity as a sin. I'd done this. Second, confess it as sin and ask God for victory over it. I did this but didn't really trust God to do it. But the last point was the clincher. Thank God for the experience that produced the self-pity. *In everything give thanks, for this is the will of God in Christ Jesus concerning you.* So, I thought, okay, God, I'll do it. But it is not going to work!

So, I started praising the Lord for everything I could think of, and slowly things were changing inside of me. The bitterness began to go away. I asked Peter to forgive me. But then the devil would put doubts in my mind, and I was right back where I was way before.

One Tuesday night, there was a baby shower at Bev Osborne's home, and Judy Bruns gave the devotions praising the

Lord for what Christ was doing in her life. At this point, I thought I couldn't stand to hear those words, "Praise the Lord" one more time. I've been doing it all week, and nothing is happening. It is getting worse. But of course, my heart attitude wasn't right. Then Lois Parks was asked to pray before we had the refreshments. Do you know how she began to pray? You guessed it. "Lord, we praise you for . . ." I felt like standing up and screaming. I can't stand to hear that again. All this time, God was working, and I was getting more miserable because I was praising God. Yet, I hadn't yielded my self-will to God to let Him have His perfect way in me.

A friend, Virginia Rydman, invited the children and me to Portland, Oregon. I decided to accept the invitation and go there for three days. Thinking maybe this "praise" idea would go away. So, we went. But you can't run away from God because He is everywhere. When I came back, I couldn't stand my misery any longer. I had been making Peter miserable; I was miserable, and everyone around me was miserable!

I had to talk to Peter again and get things straightened out. I asked him to forgive me for my bitterness, and he did. I asked God to forgive me. And He does every time. It was a joy to be in that class the following week, where people were praising God. I felt like it, too, but I couldn't seem to get my mouth open. One thing you cannot do for long is praise the Lord and live in self-pity. The two just don't mix. It is good to feel the joy and peace of God again flooding through my life. I can now praise the Lord with the right heartfelt attitude.

Chapter 5

Fear

F ear struck my heart as Paul, my youngest son, told me what his doctor told him. For several years, Paul had been bothered by blackouts, dizzy spells, and panic attacks. After his train accident at college, the doctor said Paul would someday experience problems that may require corrective surgery. Now, "someday" had finally arrived. I was not prepared for the kind of surgery that was going to happen. *It was brain surgery.*

All I remembered was what seemed to me to be horror stories of how friends' or relatives' surgery had gone. How they had left the patient awake while they drilled a hole in their head. Not only were they awake, but there was no painkiller! Others were awake while they drilled the hole—the cold feel of the vibration while the doctor sawed into their head.

Fear is not rational. It grips our emotions like a vice until we can no longer think rationally or logically or without any kind of reasoning. It blocks out all thinking based on fact. It brings unreasonable worry. Sometimes, breathing is abnormal, and chest pains, as well as stomach problems, occur.

The doctor said Paul would have surgery on August 13, 2003. He said Paul would live and be a vegetable, die, or walk out of the hospital. We were dreading this surgery. I asked everyone I knew to pray with me and for Paul. Daily, when people asked about Paul and his upcoming surgery, I would burst into tears. I couldn't stop the tears; I couldn't seem to get a grip on the fear. I couldn't let Paul go. I couldn't give him up. I knew he was on loan from God, but I couldn't face the fear of his never coming home again. A thirty-three percent chance of survival is not very good odds.

For weeks, my focus was on fear. I would wake up at night and early in the morning. I just couldn't imagine a life without Paul, our youngest son—age thirty-two, gone. He brought so much joy into our lives. His zest for *life*! What about Christy, Camden, and Madeline? They needed a husband and father.

I know in my head that the Word of God says, *In everything give thanks for this is the will of God in Christ Jesus.* But getting it from my head to my heart—how would I do that? I knew all the right words. I knew the formula I had taught over a hundred times. *Thou wilt keep him in perfect peace whose mind is stayed upon Thee (Isaiah 26:3),* This was the verse that God always brings back to me again and again since Paul was two and had meningitis. We were told then that he might die and that he had a 50/50 chance of making it. *Cast all your cares upon Him because He cares for you (I Peter 5:7).* Or, from the New English Bible, *You can throw the full weight of your anxieties upon Him because you are His personal concern.*

Jesus wanted to be my burden bearer, but I was willing to suffer and carry them myself and be absolutely miserable. Why would I choose this over the "peace that passes all understanding?

As the days grew closer to August 13, my fears increased. I was more miserable than I had been in years. What was the worst thing that could happen? He could die and be immediately with Jesus! But what about those of us left behind with the hole in our hearts that he left? What about his wife and children? Who would take care of them?

On the evening of August 12, the doctor called to say the nurse forgot to schedule the surgery and that the doctor from Children's Hospital and the machine to be used were unavailable. The surgery was rescheduled for August 30. Both Paul and I were greatly relieved. He was not looking forward to it either.

During the next two weeks, I gradually gave Paul up to God. By the time the day of the surgery arrived, I was able to cast all my anxieties on God, to trust Him for whatever happens, and to know that He would do what was best for our family.

Paul had about twenty surgeries since he was two when he had the first one, but I've never experienced this kind of unreasonable fear before. But God knows what He is doing when He puts us in positions where there's nothing we can do but trust Him, yield to Him, and let Him be God and Sovereign Lord over all. He can be trusted! He can do for us what we can never do for ourselves.

God is the light in our darkness. He is the wisdom we need in every and all situations. He wants us to trust Him with all our might and not lean on our own understanding. When He brings dark days into our lives, it shows what is really in our hearts. It shows me what I'm made of. It shows me what's in my heart and my true motives. It shows me the areas of my life I need to change and get rid of—the things that don't really matter. Fear takes away joy. Fear brings out a host of other sins. Fear makes Satan happy because it takes away our peace. Fear removes the health from our countenance and fills our hearts with foreboding and dread.

Through this, I learned that God could be trusted and obeyed. I also discovered how many people loved and cared for me and my family. They demonstrated this with prayers, cards, calls, food, and gifts. I also learned that I am not fighting against flesh and blood but against our enemy, Satan.

Only God can be relied on. Only God can fully satisfy and take away my fears, whatever they might be. Some people turn to drugs, alcohol, reading, TV, sex, sports, and anything that will help them escape their fears. But nothing satisfies like the Lord Jesus Christ. Only studying God's Word can renew our minds, and casting all our anxieties on Him in prayer can give us the peace we need.

We praise God today because Paul is still with us in the land of the living. He was back to work six days after his surgery. He's a walking miracle of the grace and the mercy of God. We give thanks, not just because Paul is still alive, but because God asks us to. It's part of God's will for us. It's called *faith*, and it comes before we see an answer to our prayers, *not after!* It's another test in our walk with God to see if we will be obedient when not knowing the outcome. It's a wrestling match with God before we see the answer and allow God's peace that passes all understanding to flood our lives.

Chapter 6

David

It was October 31, 2001. The phone rang. It was Mark calling from Minneapolis. He said, "The baby's dead." What pain struck my heart as I heard those words! The baby died while still in the womb.

Mark and Angela had called in May, just before going to Royal Servants Training Camp, to tell us they were expecting a baby in January. We were so excited for them and excited for us –our sixth grandchild! From the moment Mark told us, I just knew in my heart that the baby was a boy. Mark kept saying it might be a girl, but I knew he would be a boy.

Our friends, the Andersons, gave us frequent flyer tickets, and we could fly out on the "red-eye" flight two days after we heard. We arrived in Minneapolis on Saturday morning, November 3. I spent the day with Angela and Peter and helped Mark paint a house. On Sunday, we went to Andover, where Angela's parents live. We went to church with them. Angela's sister was there too. The pastor spoke on death and heaven. How appropriate for those whose hearts were breaking. The pastor's brother had just died three weeks earlier. Death and heaven were very much on his heart, too.

On Sunday evening, Mark and Angela prepared to go to the hospital. The doctor was going to give Angela something to start the labor process. Peter and I spent the evening alone at Mark and Angela's, waiting for the phone to ring.

On Monday morning, the baby still had not arrived. At 3:00 pm, the doctor decided to strip the membranes. Mark came out and told us to come upstairs in thirty minutes, so we did. We could tell she was in labor by the time we got there. She skipped the two transition times, and in forty-five minutes, David Paul was stillborn on November 5, 2001, at two pounds and fourteen ounces and fourteen inches long, with black hair and a button nose. But he never opened his eyes. The Chinese count time from the moment of conception. And if that's the case David Paul English was now seven months old.

After David was cleaned up, I held my sixth grandchild as the tears streamed down my face. I had prayed for him almost every day from the moment I knew of his coming. I loved him without meeting him, sight unseen. Maybe because he was English flesh and blood, he was part of our family.

I didn't know that it could be so hard to lose a grandchild that I only met once. But he will forever be in our hearts until we meet him again in heaven.

How can I give thanks when my heart is breaking? First, because God asks me to do this. If God asks me to do something, He will give me the grace to obey Him, even with joy. God is *my* refuge and *my* strength, a very present help in times of trouble (ref. Psalm 46:1). He has told me in His Word to give thanks in all things and that all things work together for good to those who love God and are called according to His purpose. Good means beneficial, and God also promises to be the God of all comfort. He will, and he has been our family's comfort through all of this for us, for Connie and Duane, and most of all for Mark and Angela.

We have seen God's people, both near and far, write letters, send cards, money, and meals, and most of all, their prayers for our family have poured out on us. We have seen God use Mark and Angela minister to others who have gone through similar circumstances. Because of their loss, they can minister to the loss of others and truly understand what they are going through.

I didn't know it would be so hard going through the holidays. Whenever baby Jesus was mentioned or lines from "Silent Night" with the words "sleep in heavenly peace," it would trigger me to cry. I've probably not cried so much in a lifetime as I've cried in the last two and a half months. Tears for Mark and Angela and their loss of a child, tears for us, and tears for Connie and Duane at our loss of a grandchild. Tears for the loss of our four babies over fifty years ago, and we didn't even give them names—tears for all those I don't even know and the children they have lost.

Why these things happen, we will only know when we get to heaven. Why do people who long for children and don't get them and those who don't want them yet seem to have them in abundance? I don't know. Mark and Angela had hoped for many children, and because of not starting their family until their thirties, they are wondering if they will have any children at all. But our God, who is great and mighty and promises to meet every need we have, will meet Mark and Angela's longing for children. How? I don't know. When? I don't know that either.

But I do know He meets and satisfies our every need as we look to Him for our supply. He is able to do exceedingly abundantly above all we could ask or think. He is able to comfort in a way no one can and with His Word. He is able to bring good out of tragedy. Why? Because God is love.

OUR LITTLE BOY

I am just a little boy that didn't quite make it there.
I have gone to be with Jesus and I am waiting for you there.
If I had lived on earth, I might have lived a life of sin.
But because I am here with Jesus, I'm still all pure within.

Author Unknown

Chapter 7

Cancer

A nother event that had a great effect on my life was in 1986. I was diagnosed with rectal cancer. I went to the doctor for a checkup for a previous hemorrhoid surgery. This was on January 31, 1986. As he examined me, he said, "I think you have cancer. Because the cancer is doubling daily, you will have to have surgery a week from today."

"Okay," I said. As I sat there waiting for my daughter to come and pick me up, I began to look back over my life to see if I was ready to go. And yes, I was. I wondered if this would be the time I would go to heaven. It was very hard to tell my family. When I told them, they were very angry. Didn't God know what was best? Didn't He always do the right thing? Now, I had the opportunity to put into practice all the things I had always taught. I found out He could be trusted. I saw how faithful God could be during this time. Mom, who was still not a believer, got to see the family of God in action because she was at my house a lot during that time. One person prayed for my joy, which was abundant during those first days home from the hospital.

We didn't have any medical insurance at that time. But people gave. My whole hospital bill was paid. It was the time of year when work was slow and finances were short, but God abundantly supplied food that lasted four months, and our cupboards were bulging. Someone else paid our house payment. Someone else took me to doctor appointments and a nutritionist and paid the bill. Mom would say, "I wonder what God is going to do today?" It was causing her to see that the God I served was an abundant God who cared about me and provided for my needs.

I also had opportunities during this time to share the Gospel with family members who were not willing to listen before. As I shared with them, I asked, "Do you want to hear the good news first or the bad news?" They always picked the good news, and I was able to share with them about the Lord Jesus Christ. My brother-in-law, Tom, sat there and cried like a baby as I shared these things with him. It wasn't too long after that that someone else led him to the Lord.

One of the most difficult things that I was going through at this time, more than the cancer surgery, was that I had a child who was rebelling. In all my Christian life, I don't ever remember experiencing the feeling of despair that came as my child began to walk away from God. A Scripture I read often during this time as I lay recovering was Psalms 27:13–14.

I would have despaired unless I had believed that I would see the goodness of the Lord in the land of the living. Wait for the Lord; be strong, and let your heart take courage; yes, wait for the Lord. (NASB)

It was probably about a year, but this child did come back to walk with God. During this trial, Peter and I began praying together for our children each day.

At first, I couldn't even pray, and Peter would have to pray for me and this child. Someone gave me Psalms and Proverbs on tape. I was able to listen to them as I went to sleep each night. They were such a comfort to me. God's Word truly does bring healing. On my first Sunday back to church, when we had our singing time, we sang, *Because He Lives, I can face tomorrow, because He lives, all fear is gone, because I know who holds the future and life is worth the living, just because He lives.*

My God is sufficient for any and all occasions. I only hit a few of the highlights of God's faithfulness in my life. He is faithful in *every* situation. Because He loves us, he will not do anything that is not for our very best. He wants our fellowship and worship. Often, He will do whatever is necessary to get our attention. In Romans 2:4 it says, *The lovingkindness of God leads us to repentance.* And it is true.

One of my favorite songs is:

He Giveth More Grace

He giveth more grace when the burdens grow greater,
He sendeth more strength when the labors increase;
To added affliction, He addeth His mercies,
To multiplied trials His multiplied peace.
When we have exhausted our store of endurance,
When our strength is gone ere the day is half done.
When we reach the end of our hoarded resources,
Our Father's full giving is only begun.
His love has no limit, His grace has no measure,
His power no boundary known unto men;
For out of His infinite riches in Jesus,
He giveth, and giveth, and giveth again.

~ Annie Johnson Flint

Fear not, for I am with you;
Be not dismayed, for I am your God.
I will strengthen you,
Yes, I will help you,
I will uphold you
with My righteous right hand.'
Isaiah 41:10

Chapter 8

Oma

From the first time Peter brought me to his parent's home, his mother disliked me. While we were dating, Peter wanted to introduce me to his family—he still lived at home. From the back of the house, I could hear his mother screaming, "How dare you bring that woman into my house without an invitation!" I was twenty at the time but looked about fourteen. She had never seen me or previously talked to me. The tone of her voice made me feel like some dance hall girl. Looking back now, I think she must have been hurting to dislike me so much when she hadn't even met me.

On January 29, 1991, Thomas, my brother-in-law, called, telling me the symptoms Oma had. I told him she was having a stroke. You need to call 911! He said Oma didn't want to go anywhere tonight. I told him if he didn't take her, she would die. He finally called 911, and she went to St. Peter's Hospital. She was there until April 7. After she was brought home from the hospital, she needed daily care. Tom had to go to work each day. My mother, Becky, Mary, and I took turns each day to care for her. I went every other day, and they went the other three days.

Taking care of Oma every day was difficult. She always felt that we owed it to her and never really appreciated anything we did. Daily, we fixed her meals and Tom's dinner as well. We cleaned her house, gave her a shower, helped her dress, and did her physical exercises with her. Eventually, she was out of the wheelchair and able to do some things on her own.

One day, Tom called and said, "You know I have a life to live, and Mom can move in with you." I asked Oma if she'd rather live in a rest home or our home. She said she would rather live at our house. This really surprised me because she never did like me.

In June 1992, Oma moved in with us. This changed our whole way of life and routine. Everything had to revolve around her care. Because she was diabetic, she had to eat all her meals on time. She also had to have meals low in sugar and carbohydrates and high in protein. She had to have blood tests each morning, shower, and help to clean her room. I could never be gone more than four hours at a time because of her meals. We could never be out later than 10:00 pm because that's when she went to bed and was afraid to be in bed when no one was in the house.

Life with Oma was not easy. If she didn't like the food, she would flush it down the toilet when no one was looking, and then it would overflow. But she never admitted to doing it. She always blamed it on someone else, even if no one else was home. She started going to the bathroom in her pants because she was too lazy to walk to the bathroom or use the commode in her room and unwilling to use the *Depends*.

I so longed to have her come to know Jesus, but she was always against it. She seemed to pride herself on the fact that she had *not* yielded to the Lord. When Kyle, her grandson, asked if she was a Christian, she said, "No, I'm not," with a big smile on her face.

We took her to church a few times, but she seemed very angry when we did. We invited many Christians to our home, and they shared the Word with her. But the look on her face when she heard the Word, or the salvation message was pure anger. But she always stayed and listened, which constantly amazed me. But she can never say, "I never heard the Gospel."

One thing I learned while caring for Oma was that she wasn't rejecting me all those years. She rejected me because I took her son. She planned that her three boys would never get married and leave her alone. She wanted her sons all to herself. It wasn't personal, and it wasn't just me. It was anyone that stood between her and her boys. I had to remember that I wasn't fighting against flesh and blood or Oma herself but against principalities and powers in the unseen world.

I prayed daily for me and for her. I had to depend on God, or I would quit in a minute. I always prayed that I could do it one more day because today was all I had. I wanted to honor God in the way that I cared for her.

I was able to give thanks to God for slowing me down. I couldn't go to a lot of places and do things I wanted because I'd have to hire someone to take my place. This would be very expensive. I did hire someone once a week all day so I could teach my class, run errands, buy groceries, or have lunch with a friend. I appreciated those days out. When I returned home, I found I could care for Oma better. Because I had a break, my outlook improved.

I cannot say I enjoyed caring for Oma, but I could give thanks for the lessons God taught me while caring for her. She was probably the most selfish person I've ever known. Oma thought we should find great pleasure in anything we could do for her. She thought we had been created to serve her. But she never thought of doing anything for anyone else.

A friend of mine, Bev, was Oma's caregiver on Tuesdays when I ran errands. She spent two hours with her in two separate weeks and shared the Word of God with her. Because she liked Bev so much, Oma even went through the motions of accepting the Lord. The next day, I asked Oma if she wanted me to read the Bible to her. Because of her diabetes, she couldn't see well enough to read. Oma said, "Why would I want to hear the Bible?" She had only wanted to please Bev, which is why she prayed with her.

After eight years of caring for her, we placed her in a Christian home for two years. They loved and cared for her, but she was still not open to the Gospel. When we visited her, she ignored us. Maybe she was trying to get back at us for putting her there. The Christian home closed, so we placed her in another rest home. This time, she was glad to see us when we visited. Why, I don't know. She even initiated the conversation. My greatest hope for her was that she would be saved before going into eternity.

Oma died at the age of eighty-one. I cried and cried at her funeral service because she rejected the Gospel so many times. This brought me great sadness. I knew I had done all I could to take care of her. This must be how God feels when He does so much for mankind, and they reject Him over and over because people want it their way instead of His.

Jesus said to him,
"I am the way, the truth, and the life.
No one comes to the Father
except through Me.
John 14:6

The harvest is past,
The summer is ended,
And we are not saved!"
Jeremiah 8:2o

Look to Me, and be saved,
All you ends of the earth!
For I am God, and there is no other.
Isaiah 45:22

Chapter 9

Two Strokes and a Fall

A few months ago, I was asked to give the devotions to a group of women—divorced, widowed, and single. The group was called *Connections*. My subject was *In Everything Give Thanks*. In March 2024, I was given the opportunity to live out these words—*once again.*

Earlier this year, my daughter Becky and my son Paul told me they were taking me to Disneyland to celebrate my eightieth birthday. Our family has always liked going to Disneyland together. Our painting business slowed yearly during the winter. It was nice in California at this time of year, so that we would go after Christmas every few years.

On Sunday, March 10, the missions team at our church was hosting a brunch for a visiting missionary from Israel. I was to be at the church at 8:00 am to set up tables and chairs with the rest of the team. When I got there, I felt very strange. I couldn't speak very well. When I did speak, the words didn't come out right. One of the pastor's wives said, "You look like you should sit down." All I could do was nod my head, "Yes." Then another person on the mission team said, "Kathie, are you okay? I shook my head. "No." "What's wrong?" I was finally able to tell her I forgot to take my medicine before I came. She said, "I'm taking you home right away so you can take your medicine." She had never been to my house before, and I had a hard time speaking to her so I could tell her how to get there. All I could do was point and say, "Here." We finally got there and then drove back to the church. By the time the brunch was over I felt okay— almost. But I felt something wasn't quite right. After church, I drove myself home. I took a very long nap. That was my first heart stroke.

When I first got up the following day, I knew something was wrong. I knew I needed to go to the emergency room. I called my son Paul and told him what I was going through, and he came right away. He took me took me to Kaiser-Permanente, my medical facility that had an emergency room. After many tests, they decided I was probably having a stroke.

Immediately, they sent me across the street to St. Peter's Hospital. They wouldn't let Paul drive me even though it was half a block away. So Paul met me there. A stroke team of six people was waiting for me as the ambulance people wheeled me in. They started running all kinds of tests. When they took my blood pressure, it was up to 222. The nurse looked nervous when I said, "Is that my blood pressure?" She didn't think I could see that far across the room. I was still in the hallway because they had no available rooms. Everyone was running around looking for the doctor. This was my second stroke.

After four days in the hospital, different specialists visited me: the speech therapist, occupational therapist, and heart specialist. The heart specialist told me I had a stroke. They said there are three different kinds: transient ischemic attack, ischemic stroke (the kind I had), and hemorrhagic stroke (the kind where you can't walk or talk). The speech therapist said when she did some tests with me that I recognized my mistakes when I spoke or wrote (perhaps because I journal every day), and I was writing the same way I was talking, even saying words that didn't make any sense, that was a good sign that I was going to get better.

I didn't know when I left the hospital that they had put me on two blood thinners that were going to cause me some problems in the days ahead. When I got home from the hospital, a friend of our family came and stayed with me for three days.

On March 20 Becky, Paul, Kelly, my grandson, and I flew to California to Disneyland for six days. A friend picked us up at the airport and took us to her home for the night. The next day, she took us to Paul's friend's house, where we would stay for the next five days.

On March 22, which was my eightieth birthday, I was talking to Becky and Paul who were in the kitchen. I was in the foyer, and the sunken dining room was ahead of me. I was looking at my kids, not where I was going. I walked straight ahead and fell, hitting my knee on the ceramic tile. I flew into the dining room and ended up on my back. There on the floor, I looked up and Becky and Paul were looking down at me. At that moment, I don't remember having a lot of pain. So, we ate breakfast and went to Disneyland!

The lady we stayed with rented a wheelchair for me. The rental cost for the week was $40.00. If we rented it at Disneyland, it was $50.00 per day. That was a blessing. Also, our plane trip was free because of frequent flyer tickets. Our friends wanted us to stay with them at no charge. They also took us back and forth to Disneyland. God kept providing everything we needed.

Kelly was the one who pushed the wheelchair all day long, which was a blessing. He is always lots of fun. The weather was good – 65-75 degrees. Also, because of the wheelchair we got to go to the head of the line—all four of us.

We had a wonderful day at the park. All went well. But then the pain from my fall began to show its ugly head. I took some Ibuprofen when we returned to our friend's house that night. I didn't know it was another blood thinner. Because the pain was so bad in my leg, I took four pills.

The next morning, I began to bleed. I took more of the pills. I would have gone to the emergency room if I had been home. But I didn't want to be stuck in a California hospital. Because of the blood thinners, I was freezing all the time. I had four shirts, a coat, and a blanket while in the wheelchair, even though the weather was nice.

Because it was my birthday, they gave me a button that said, "Happy Birthday" with my name and age, eighty. Everywhere I went, people called out, "Happy Birthday." When the parade went by, the characters in the parade were yelling from the floats, "Happy Birthday, Kathie." I think the kids were getting a little tired of hearing that the days we were at Disneyland.

On March 26, we flew back to Washington. I knew I needed to go to the emergency room. My granddaughter Emily took me to Kaiser. They ran some tests and then sent me to St. Peter's

Hospital—again. Emily stayed with me for seven hours. Then Kayla, my other granddaughter, came and relieved her so Emily could go to work. Then my daughter Becky came, and then Paul and Kelly came.

Then, the medical staff started running different tests. I had to have a blood transfusion, and then two pints of iron, and a colonoscopy! The tests ran all night long to prepare me for a test at 9:00 am. This time, I was in the hospital for another four days. But this time, I got a room, not a bed in the hall! Even through all of this, I knew the Lord was with me. I had wonderful care at the hospital. I also had wonderful care from my loving family. God was providing whatever I needed at just the right time.

I was well taken care of when I came home from the hospital. I had so many people who came to help me in so many ways. They brought meals and flowers, cards, and food, asking how they could help. I still had a lot of pain in my leg and back. I needed a walker. My daughter Becky brought me a walker to get around the house. Because of the pain pills, I could no longer drive for a few weeks. I had to depend on others for everything. My son Mark came from Minneapolis to care for me for a week. I was so well cared for I could not complain about anything. Whatever I needed, God kept supplying. Eventually, the pain pills ran out. I couldn't take any over-the-counter painkillers. I had to learn to endure the pain.

It is now May 2024. I am starting to feel better. I was beginning to think I would have to live with this pain forever. Some days, the pain was like the last stages of labor in having a baby. But God gave me endurance even in this pain. I wanted to have a good attitude and not complain.

Our pastor was preaching on the Book of Job during this time. He talked about being "better, not bitter." I didn't want to be talking about my pain, but I wanted to talk about God. The healing has come very slowly. But each day, I could see I was getting better. When it takes time to heal, I began to appreciate how good even a "little better" feels. I could thank God for His goodness and mercy. I could have broken a leg or arm when I fell, but I didn't! I could have broken a hip and had to have surgery, but I didn't! God showed His grace to me again, giving me what I didn't deserve. I praise God for giving me a second chance to live for Him more fully. I praise Him for my healing. I praise Him for allowing me to appreciate all the little things I used to take for granted.

All my life I have had a Pollyanna outlook on life, finding something good in every situation. But after I became a Christian and read I Thessalonians 5:18, "In everything give thanks, for this is the will of God in Christ Jesus concerning you." I wanted to obey His Word. I discovered how God uses our adverse circumstances to teach us something—that He brings something good out of the difficult.

Chapter 10

Tidings of Joy

Dear family and friends, many of you know, but many of you don't know that Peter went home to be with the Lord on January 3, 2019. I miss him so much. December 4, 2019 would have been our fifty-fifth anniversary. The Bible says, *In everything give thanks, for this is the will of God in Christ Jesus concerning you (I Thessalonians 5:18)*. But how do I give thanks when the love of my life for fifty-four years has suddenly been taken away from me, and I am left alone? So, I began to look for ways I could give thanks to God for my new way of life.

The Bible also says that God would be a husband to the widow, which is what I am now. God's Word says, *And my God will supply all your needs according to His riches in glory in Christ Jesus (Philippians 4:19 NASB)*.

He also said,

Delight yourself in Him and He will give you the desires of your heart (Psalm 37:4 NASB). He also said,

And He is the stability of your times, a wealth of salvation, wisdom, and knowledge; the fear of the Lord is His treasure. Isaiah 33:6 (NASB)

Other things I can give thanks for is a long and satisfying marriage. For a husband who gave me the things I would need after he left. A smaller house that I could take care of on my own. He bought me a new car that wouldn't break down. He put money in the bank for needs that might come up. He put me in a senior community that cares for and looks out for people like me—older.

I can give thanks for four children who have been caring for me and meeting my needs before I even ask them. I have nine grandchildren who are continually visiting, texting me, and checking in to see if there is anything I need or can't do on my own.

I have a Sunday School class and other friends who continue to care for me through their prayers, cards, visits, meals, phone calls, and anything else they think would be helpful.

I have the Lord who watches over me day and night. He is nearer than hands or feet. He provides His Word for my instruction on how to live one day at a time. He will never leave me. He will provide for my every need. How can I fear the future when He is right here beside me? His Word says,

For I know the plans that I have for you, declares the Lord, plans for good and not for evil to give you a future and a hope. Then you will call upon Me and come and pray to Me, and I will listen to you. Jeremiah 29:11 ESV

When the Lord took Peter to his heavenly home and relieved him from all the pain he had suffered these past five years, that is a reason I give thanks. He no longer suffers. I can give thanks that he was a wonderful husband for fifty-four years—a good father greatly loved by all his children and grandchildren. He had seventy-five good years. He knew Jesus as His Lord and Savior and wanted others to know Him, too. He was unselfish and gave to many people, which I only learned at his memorial service. I choose to give thanks in obedience to God's Word because giving thanks and praise to God brings peace, joy, and contentment that cannot be found in any other way. Living for Jesus is the most satisfying life I can think of and has brought me great joy for the past sixty-six years. I pray that you can have this blessed hope as you give thanks to Him in all circumstances.

Hallelujah

And God will wipe away every tear
from their eyes;
there shall be no more death,
nor sorrow, nor crying.
There shall be no more pain,
for the former things have passed away."
Revelation 21:4

He Leadeth Me

He leadeth me.
In pastures green? No, not always.
Sometimes He Who knowest best
In kindness leadeth me in weary ways
Where heavy shadows be;
Out of the sunshine warm and soft and bright,
Out of the sunshine into the darkest night.
I oft would yield to sorrow and to fright
Only for this: I know He holds my hand.
So, whether led in green, or desert land
I trust, although I cannot understand.

He leadeth me.
Beside still waters? No, not always so.
Oft times the heavy tempests round me blow,
And o'er my soul the waves and billows go.
And when the storm beats wildest, and I cry
Aloud for help, the Master standeth, by
And whispers to my soul: "Lo, it is I."
Above the tempest wild I hear Him say:
"Beyond the darkness lies the perfect day;
In every path of thine I lead the way."

So whether on the hilltops, high and fair
I dwell or in the sunless valleys, where
The shadows lie—what matter? He is there
And more than this; where'er the pathway lead
He gives to me no helpless, broken read
But His Own hand, sufficient for my need.
So where He leads me I can safely go.
And in the blest hereafter I shall know
Why in His wisdom He hath led me so.

—Rev. John F. Chaplain
Public Domain

About The Author

Kathie Ann English, now eighty years of age, a mother of four children, ten grandchildren, and four great-grandchildren. A committed teacher, Kathie has taught home-school students for thirty-five years. For five years, she was a certified Bible teacher with Precept Ministries. Kathie also discipled (one-on-one) over twenty-five women, teaching them to follow Jesus Christ more fully. Actively involved in Connections, she brings encouragement from Scripture to forty-fifty women who struggle with life issues. Kathie has faithfully supported her husband and now, her son, as office manager and bookkeeper for Bavarian Painting Company for fifty-three years. Her husband, now deceased (2019), began the company in 1971. Her son, Paul, runs the company. *In Everything Give Thanks* is Kathie's first book